PENGUIN BOOKS

ON BIRTH

Timothy Keller started Redeemer Presbyterian Church in New York City with his wife, Kathy, and their three sons. Redeemer grew to nearly 5,500 regular Sunday attendees and helped to start more than three hundred new churches around the world. In 2017 Keller moved from his role as senior minister at Redeemer to the staff of Redeemer City to City, an organization that helps national church leaders around the world reach and minister in global cities. He is the author of *The Prodigal Prophet, God's Wisdom for Navigating Life*, as well as *The Meaning of Marriage, The Prodigal God*, and *The Reason for God*, among others.

T0176269

On Birth

TIMOTHY
KELLER

PENGUIN BOOKS

PENGUIN BOOKS
An imprint of Penguin Random House LLC
penguinrandomhouse.com

All Bible references are from the New International Version
(NIV), unless otherwise noted.

ISBN 9780143135357 (paperback)
ISBN 9780525507017 (ebook)

Printed in the United States of America
3rd Printing

Set in Adobe Garamond • Designed by Sabrina Bowers

To our grandchildren;
the joy we felt at your births
could only be exceeded by the knowledge
that you have experienced the new birth.

Contents

Introduction to the How to Find God Series

Life is a journey, and finding and knowing God is fundamental to that journey. When a new child is born, when we approach marriage, and when we find ourselves facing death—either in old age or much earlier—it tends to concentrate the mind. We shake ourselves temporarily free from absorption in the whirl of daily life and ask the big questions of the ages:

Am I living for things that matter?

Will I have what it takes to face this new stage of life?

Do I have a real relationship with God?

The most fundamental transition any human being can make is what the Bible refers to as the new birth (John 3:1–8), or becoming a "new creation" (2 Corinthians 5:17). This can happen at any time in a life, of course, but often the circumstances that lead us to vital faith in Christ occur during these tectonic shifts in life stages. Over forty-five years of ministry, my wife, Kathy, and I have seen that people are particularly open to exploring a relationship with God at times of major life transition.

In this series of short books we want to help readers facing major life changes to think about what constitutes the truly changed life. Our purpose is to give readers the Christian foundations for life's most important and profound moments. We start with birth and baptism, move into marriage, and conclude with death. My hope is that these slim books will provide guidance, comfort, wisdom, and, above all, will help point the way to finding and knowing God all throughout your life.

On Birth

First Birth

Born to raise us from the earth;
Born to give us second birth.

—"HARK! THE HERALD ANGELS SING,"

CHARLES WESLEY

The Christian faith teaches that every person should experience two births. In one's first birth you are born into the natural world. Then, in what Charles Wesley calls our "second birth," which Jesus himself describes as being "born again" (John 3:3), we are born into the kingdom of God and receive new spiritual life. The first birth is ours because God is our Creator; the second birth can be ours because God is also our Redeemer. The Lord is the author of both.

In light of this, we want to consider the spiritual issues surrounding both births. What does it mean to receive a new human life from God? What are the responsibilities of the family and the church to newborns? How can we help our children who are with us through the first birth come to experience the second birth?

Fearful and Wonderful

Rather than directly creating each new human being himself, the Lord bestowed on the union of male and female the unique power to bring new human beings into the world. No wonder then that newborn babies in the Bible are always regarded with wonder as signs of God's blessing. The original charge of God to the human race was: "Be fruitful, and multiply and fill the earth" (Genesis 1:28). While God does not demand that all people be married, as Jesus himself and Saint Paul demonstrate, nevertheless, Genesis 1:28 explains why we feel so deeply that we are witnessing a miracle of God when gazing on a newborn child. Psalm 127:3 says that *all* children are a "reward" from God.

But there is another side to it.

God often sends heroes and deliverers into the world by giving them as newborns to couples who are disconsolate because they cannot have children. So Isaac, Jacob, Joseph, Samson, and Samuel are all born to women who previously could not conceive. And yet a quick survey of their lives, particularly those of Jacob, Joseph, and Samson, reveals that these children, who were direct "gifts of God," were also great heart-griefs to their parents.

Something of this is seen in this famous passage in Psalm 139:13–16: "For you created my inmost being; you knit me together in my mother's womb. I praise you because I am *fearfully and wonderfully* made . . . Your eyes saw my unformed body; all the days ordained for me were written in your book." As one Bible scholar put it: "Our pre-natal fashioning by God [is] a powerful reminder of the value He sets on us, even as embryos, and of His planning our end from the beginning."[1]

The phrase we are "fearfully and wonderfully made" is full of interest. Every baby born into the world is a wonderful creation, but at the same time a frightening one. Anyone who looks

on a newborn—realizing this is a new human
life in the image of the Creator, come into the
world along with particular gifts and callings
and a life planned by the Lord of history —must
respond with a kind of fear and trembling. And
no one should behold a child with more awe
and fear than the child's parents.

When Kathy and I brought home our first-
born, I was surprised to see her cuddle him
close and weep. Partly this was her hormones
talking, she said, but partly it was a recognition
of what we had let this tiny little person in for
as a member of a fallen race. Yes, "all the days
ordained for him" were "written in God's book,"
but as an adult she knew that our son's book
would contain disappointment, hurt, failure, pain,
loss, and ultimately his own death. All this would
happen no matter how hard we would try to

shield him. So she literally trembled before the responsibility of being a parent to this wonder of the universe. And when I thought about it, so did I.

Kathy concluded:

> The birth of a child has been referred to by one mother as a "family-quake." Whether it is joyful and desired or not, the first or fourteenth, healthy or challenged, a new person entering the world alters history in ways both large and small just by reason of his or her existence. As a new parent, you have entered a fellowship stretching back millennia, one that includes queens and slaves, thirteen-year-olds in ancient cultures and at least one ninety-year-old mother, Sarah, mother of Isaac, in the Bible. Every

kingdom, tribe, tongue, and nation has
its rituals surrounding giving birth, and
for a reason. It is a near-mystical event,
welcoming a person who was not-there
but now *is*.

Blessing or Burden?

Bringing new life into the world is the most tre-
mendous, astonishing thing a human being can
do. Women are especially given the privilege of
receiving and nurturing new life, being subcre-
ators with God. In willingly receiving the em-
brace of the masculine, the power granted to
the female sex is unleashed, and new, formerly
nonexistent life blooms into the world.[2] Not
only does the creation of new life propel civilization and culture into the next generation in

its myriad forms; it also changes those of us in the current generation in countless ways, demanding sacrifice on a scale you may never before have attempted.

But modern people are ambivalent about this immense privilege, to say the least.

The fear (if not the wonder) of children is something modern people see very clearly. We live in a society that has seen a sharp decline in the birth rate, to the point that there are not enough births to replace deaths—the so-called replacement rate. Fewer people today see children as a blessing.

Liberals tend to blame economic factors and conservatives tend to point to the rising tide of selfishness. One of the better books about this is *All Joy and No Fun: The Paradox of Modern Parenthood* by Jennifer Senior, because the author is careful not to overgeneralize. She lists numerous reasons for the contemporary ambivalence toward parenting, but two stand out.

The first is the unprecedented emphasis in modern culture on personal autonomy and self-realization. We have more freedom to choose our careers, our sexual practices, our geographical location, whether to marry and stay married, whether to have children or not. "Few of us would want to reverse the historical advance that gave us our newfound freedoms," she writes, but we have "come to define liberty negatively, as lack of dependence, the right not to be obligated to others . . . [and] to mean immunity from social claims on one's wealth or time."[3]

Because we strongly conceive of liberty as freedom from obligation, "parenthood is a dizzying shock." We have now been given the right to choose or change anything that does not seem to be satisfying or benefiting us—job, location, career, spouse. "But we can never choose or change our children. They are the last binding obligation in a culture that asks for almost no other permanent commitments at all."[4]

I don't think the "dizzying shock" to parents can simply be read as rank selfishness. Rather, parenting challenges all the habits of the heart that our culture has formed in us around relationships. Changing those habits is neither easy nor simple.

The other reason that modern parenthood is so paradoxical is that parents pour more emotional and financial capital into raising their children than ever, so much so that parenting "may have become . . . its own profession, so to speak." There is only one problem with this job: "its goals are far from clear." What are parents trying to actually *do* with their children? For example, "today's parents are . . . charged with the psychological well-being of their sons and daughters, which on the face of it is a laudable goal. But it's a murky one."[5] Indeed—who defines "psychological well-being"? Does it simply mean happiness? Can't cruel people be happy? Then is the goal to make them moral and good? Even though contemporary parents may want that, they live in a culture that insists moral values are culturally constructed. And usually people throw in that we should not impose our values on our children but let them choose their own. Really? Should we not care if they are not becoming honest, compassionate, fair dealing, and patient? Are those things we can let them choose—or not?

Christians have resources that speak directly to these challenges. To begin with, the biblical teaching about human nature reframes parental expectations. Modern child psychology literature—and more popular, informal folk wisdom about parenting—always, inevitably, assumes some philosophical anthropology, some view of human nature that underlies everything else. It may be positive about our ability to shape our lives through our own choices or pessimistic about it. It may see human nature as basically good or as irremediably bad. The Bible, however, tells us that human beings are far greater *and* worse than we can imagine. We are made in God's image but deeply marred by our own sin. As C. S. Lewis's main character says to the human children in his *Chronicles of Narnia*:

> "You come of the Lord Adam and the Lady Eve," said Aslan. "And that is both honor enough to erect the head of the poorest beggar, and shame enough to

bow the shoulders of the greatest em-
peror on earth. Be content."[6]

This Christian view of human nature helps parents learn from—without fully accepting—a
host of more reductionistic approaches to child
development. There is more "conservative" literature that stresses things like discipline, limits,
and the teaching of moral values, as well as
more "progressive" materials that emphasize listening to children, strong affirmation, and giving them freedom to question and think for
themselves. The Christian view of human beings as fallen bearers of the divine image can
borrow from and learn from all of them without embracing their more simplistic views of the
human heart.

Beyond this critical understanding of human

nature, Christianity gives us other resources that directly address the challenges that parents have always felt and feel today.

Giving Your Child

Children are a joy, but parents often sense a responsibility that can be overwhelming. The Christian church offers, in response, the sacrament of baptism.[7] While not all Christians practice infant baptism, most have some way of publicly dedicating their children to God, which follows the Jewish practice. After Jesus's birth we are told: "Joseph and Mary took him to Jerusalem to present him to the Lord" (Luke 2:22).

When we bring our children to God in baptism, it does not confer salvation automatically on the child. Just as God does not magically create new human beings but does it through the union of a man and a woman, so he normally brings about our second birth much like our first birth—through love relationships and, so often, through the family.

Sin tends to run in families. We see weaknesses in our parents and grandparents that show up in us even though we dislike the traits, even when we try with all our might to avoid them. But *grace* tends to run in families, too. Love and good models of faith and grace can lead a child to seek those things for himself or herself.

Baptizing your child is an enormous help to parents. It is a public service with vows, surrounded by friends in the Christian church community. Modern people have virtually abandoned public promises (except for weddings)—and they therefore have neglected a powerful mechanism for shaping character. To make solemn promises before the faces of family and friends molds us and makes permanent impressions on our minds, hearts, and wills.

In baptism parents take binding, covenantal oaths. We promise to grow in grace ourselves (see "Growing in Grace") in order to attract our children not so much to us but to our Savior and Lord. We promise to bring the child up not in isolation but in the midst of a church community that is united by promises to God and one another. Ordinarily those surrounding us at baptism make verbal public vows to support us and care for our children as well. Our community rallies around us and we feel reinforced for the calling and mission of parenthood. And while baptism may not save the child, we believe real divine grace and strength from God comes down in response to these vows, as our God is a covenant God who honors promises (Psalm 56:12–13).

There are almost as many sets of baptismal parental promises as there are denominations, but one set always has stood out to us:

To the Parents

1. Do you acknowledge that you are saved only through faith in Jesus, not through anything you have done or ever will do, but only through His finished work—His death upon the Cross—by which He took upon Himself the penalty for your sins?

2. Do you realize that baptism is not a saving ordinance, and though it signifies your child's membership in the covenant community, it is not a matter of magic? Do you understand that your child is responsible to receive Christ as Savior and Lord as she [or he] becomes accountable to Him?

3. Have you covenanted with God to give back this child to Him, so that, if He sees fit in His providence to call this child home to Himself, you will not complain against Him, or if she [or he] grows to adulthood and is called to serve God in a faraway place, you will not stand in her [or his] way but rather encourage her [or him]?

4. Do you in this sacrament covenant together with God to raise your child in the instruc-

tion, obedience, and worship of the Lord, to pray for and with her [or him], to keep her [or him] in the fellowship of God's people, to be faithful and loving in your home, to be godly examples of faith yourselves, and therefore to do your utmost to lead her [or him] to a saving knowledge of Christ?

To the Congregation

Do you, the members of this congregation, agree to pray for these parents as they raise their children in the Christian faith, and to support them in their efforts by providing their children with further examples of obedience and service to God? Should these parents neglect their God-given task, will you in all humility rebuke and correct them?[8]

Raising Your Child

Dedicating your child to God through public promises before the congregation directs parents to a number of practices that are designed to turn a child's heart toward God. Western secular culture presents many unique challenges to Christian parents who want to do this.

Our society's cultural institutions hold many faith assumptions about human nature and morality, yet secular people generally do not recognize them as beliefs at all. We absorb the reigning narratives of the culture through commercials, movies and TV episodes, social media, and innumerable other forms—"You have to be true to yourself"; "You have to do what makes you happy and not sacrifice it"; "You should be free to live as you choose as long as you harm no one else"; "No one has the right to tell

anyone else what is right or wrong for them";
"You have to live your own truth." Each of
these statements is at sharp variance with biblical teaching on discipleship, on sin and grace,
and on the character of God. Every one of them
assumes highly debatable beliefs about human
purpose and identity, yet they are presented
as beyond question—as being simply objective,
reasonable, open-minded, and scientific. Social
theorists call this "mystification"—creating the
impression that contestable arguments are really
unassailable facts about reality.

A good example of this can be seen in a
New York Times Magazine article about sex. The
writer says that for centuries traditional societ-
ies "condemned as aberrant sexual pleasures we
now know are healthy."[9] But those older cultures did not think that the sexual practices
were "unhealthy"—rather, that they were wrong.

They were making moral judgments. The writer, however, does not say that "now we know that there are no moral norms regarding sex"—even though that is what she means. Instead the author cloaks her beliefs about sex, which are in many ways a throwback to the beliefs of ancient Greco-Roman culture, in the language of science.

Parents who want to see their child's heart turn toward Christ and his gospel must come to grips with the ways that the culture mystifies its beliefs as commonsense truths. Young people daily spend hours on social media, where immersive waves of stories, testimonies, movies, videos, commercials, and music convey a worldview of secular modernity.

If you think that merely taking a child to church or sending them to a youth group once a week will be sufficient to overcome all this and form them as thoughtful Christians, you are wrong. What will most likely happen is that inwardly their deepest habits of the heart and instinctive ways of judgment will become disconnected from the Bible stories they still publicly profess. At some point in their late teens or college years, Christianity will begin to seem implausible.

What can parents do? James D. Hunter is a sociologist who has studied "character formation" curricula used in schools across the United States. Each curriculum seeks to produce honesty, justice, kindness, generosity, wisdom, self-control, and other virtues in students. However, Hunter shows that all the various courses and materials, whether used in public or private schools, secular or religious schools, show no evidence that they actually produce character change in pupils.[10]

Martin Luther King, Jr., is regularly lifted up by these curricula as a model of the virtue of justice, and students are exhorted to emulate him. But, Hunter asks, how did Martin Luther King, Jr., become the man he became? He was the product of a rich and strong community, the African-American church, which gave its people not just ethical principles, but a "cosmology." This is a way to understand the universe through the story of the God of the book of Exodus, the God who liberates. This story was not taught by the church as simply an inspirational account of something that happened in the past, but rather as a story that explains all of history and in which people can live today.

In short, what produced a Martin Luther

King, Jr., was a robust community that actually incarnated and lived out a clear moral vision, based on a set of beliefs about where the world came from, who human beings are, and where they are going.[11] Obviously classrooms cannot produce all this, but families can, especially if they are embedded in a particular church community.

Hunter calls this a moral ecology. It consists of mutually reinforcing communities in which the children live, such as church and home (and sometimes also school), where a particular vision and story of the world, and of the moral values that flow from it, are taught, explained, embodied, and applied to daily life. The features of such a shaping community always include a moral cosmology and sourcebook, as well as moral discourse, imagination, and modeling.

A Moral Ecology

In Deuteronomy 6 the Bible gives us a glimpse of the moral ecology that Christian parents must inhabit with their children if they are to be formed as thoughtful Christians with gospel-based moral character. The beginning of the chapter provides the goal of character formation.

> These are the commands, decrees and laws the LORD your God directed me to teach you to observe in the land that you are crossing the Jordan to possess, so that you, your children and their children after them may fear the LORD your God as long as you live by keeping all his decrees and commands that I give you, and so that you may enjoy long life. Hear, Israel, and be careful to

> obey so that it may go well with you
> and that you may increase greatly in a
> land flowing with milk and honey, just
> as the LORD, the God of your ancestors,
> promised you. (Deuteronomy 6:1–3)

The goal is not just ethical behavior ("keep all his decrees and commands") but also an inner awe and wonder toward the greatness of God ("the fear of the Lord"). This is a changed heart, not mere behavioral compliance. What is needed are habits of the heart in which we find God the greatest source of our meaning, identity, hope, and happiness. How can such a heart be nurtured?

Moral principles only make sense if they are grounded in a *moral cosmology*—a picture of a universe that supports them. Here we see that if we obey his commandments "it [will] go well with you" and "you may enjoy long life" (verse 3). The God of the Bible is our loving Creator, who has designed us for serving, knowing, and loving God and our neighbor. So to obey the laws of our Creator is not only to honor him but also to honor our own design, just as a fish does when it lives in the water rather than on land or the way a car owner does when she follows the owner's manual.

In this community there is also the *moral sourcebook*, the Bible. The book of Deuteronomy is a series of sermons by Moses for the community of God's people. The divinely revealed Ten Commandments are laid out in chapter 5, and then in chapter 6 Moses says that it is "these commandments" that "are to be on your hearts" and impressed on your children. The Christian church, of course, has more than

Deuteronomy—it has the entire Bible as its sourcebook for practical moral wisdom.

In this community there is also what Hunter calls *moral discourse.* It is not sufficient to put the moral rules up on the whiteboard and have students memorize them. As the chapter says, you must "talk about them when you sit at home and when you walk along the road, when you lie down and when you get up" (verse 7). Applying the rules to concrete daily life takes much wisdom and constant attention. We must look at the numerous choices we make every day and ask: "What is the right thing to do in this situation?" You must talk to your children about why a particular decision or action that day fits in with what we know of Jesus and his gospel. We have to show children that God's commands are not just something you believe in the abstract but are to be "on your hands and . . . on your foreheads" (verse 8). We are to show how your daily thoughts ("foreheads") and actions ("hands") are shaped by your faith and experience of Christ.

In this community there is *moral imagination*. Alasdair MacIntyre's classic *After Virtue* shows that moral character has for centuries been instilled most powerfully by stories that embody and illustrate moral qualities.[12] Stories from our own community's past can be most formative of all.

> In the future, when your son asks you, "What is the meaning of the stipulations, decrees and laws the LORD our God has commanded you?" tell him: "We were slaves of Pharaoh in Egypt, but the LORD brought us out of Egypt with a mighty

hand. Before our eyes the LORD sent signs and wonders—great and terrible—on Egypt and Pharaoh and his whole household. But he brought us out from there to bring us in and give us the land he promised on oath to our ancestors. The LORD commanded us to obey all these decrees and to fear the LORD our God, so that we might always prosper and be kept alive, as is the case today." (Deuteronomy 6:20–24)

Notice that when children ask the big "why" question—as in "*Why* must we never lie? Never steal? Never commit adultery?"—they are not to get a lecture on moral philosophy. They are given narratives—stories of struggles between good and evil—that capture imaginations and shape hearts even more than arguments and propositions.

Hebrews 11 gives us a New Testament summary of what we might call "heroes of faith," including Abraham, Jacob, Joseph, Moses, and others. But it is important to realize that these biblical figures are not like the moral exemplars of other cultures. Abraham, Jacob, David, Peter—just to take four—were deeply flawed and had lives marked by repeated, serious moral failures. Why are these the stories we get to give our children?

It is because the gospel is the message of salvation by God's unmerited grace. Christ's salvation is not for the strong and competent and accomplished, but for those strong enough to admit they are none of these things. Instead of a series of triumphant, nearly flawless paragons of virtue, the Bible points us to weak people who don't deserve God's grace, don't seek it, and don't appreciate it even after God has given it to them anyway. The greatest recipients of grace are the biggest repenters. It is stories such as these that get across so vividly the principles and power of the gospel. Christian moral principles are dynamic implications of Jesus's saving love for us in the gospel. Doing justice, being honest, reconciling with enemies, and staying chaste are things we will *want* to do if the gospel of Jesus's costly grace is not only understood but grasped with the heart and applied to daily life.

Finally, a Christian community that is a moral ecology is characterized by *moral modeling*. In the midst of all the instructions about what we should be doing with our children, Moses says:

> Be sure to keep the commands of the LORD your God and the stipulations and decrees he has given you. Do what is

right and good in the LORD's sight.
(Deuteronomy 6:17–18)

Here is perhaps the most commonsense feature of an effective, character-forming community. Children have to see gospel-based moral values and traits actually embodied in the people around them. We must live what we believe and profess. Hypocrisy will alienate our children from us, and if it does, we will deserve it.

Kathy and I gratefully discovered that despite our mediocre parenting, our young teenage sons grew up with a very positive regard for the Christian faith. It was because they were surrounded in our New York City church with young men and women in their twenties and early thirties who were accomplished in their fields and attractive in their character, but also deeply committed believers.

Modern parenting manuals often counsel that parents not try to instill their own "values" in children but instead support them in forming their own.[13] But the fact remains that everyone else in the world—from advertisers to social media platforms to most of your child's schoolteachers—will implicitly or overtly be trying to catechize your children with its ideas such as "live your own truth." If you don't teach your children well, someone else will. If we don't form moral ecologies that shape our children into Christ-likeness, they will be shaped by the world's moral ecology.

Enduring the Sword

When Mary and Joseph took Jesus to the temple for his dedication, they met an old man,

Simeon, who by the Holy Spirit was able to discern that this child was the Messiah long promised. After his famous exclamation, "You may now dismiss your servant in peace. For my eyes have seen your salvation" (Luke 2:29–30), he then turned to Mary and prophesied:

> This child is destined to cause the falling and rising of many in Israel, and to be a sign that will be spoken against, so that the thoughts of many hearts will be revealed. And a sword will pierce your own soul too. (Luke 2:34–35)

Simeon is saying that for all the peace that Jesus will bring into the world, he will also bring conflict. His claim to be the Son of God will bring salvation and rest to many people, but others will reject it and so people will be divided over him.

And Mary in particular, as Jesus's mother, will experience both the profoundest joy at seeing the greatness of her son *and* the deepest grief as she watches his arrest, torture, and death. Of course on the far side of Jesus's resurrection it would become clear to Mary that what her son endured was for the salvation of us all. But up until that moment, her experience was not very different from what mothers, and indeed all parents, experience. Amidst the joy—a sword.

In a sense every love relationship brings "a sword in the heart," because when you love someone truly you bind your heart to the other person with the result that your happiness is tied to his or her happiness. You can't be fully happy when they are not. This heart-tying is involuntary in the case of parents, so that, as it has been said, "you can be only as happy as your unhappiest child."[14]

No wonder so many modern people have given parenting a pass. But just as Jesus could not bless the world without the suffering of his parents, so we cannot give the world the blessing of our children's new life without accepting the sword in our hearts. We should bear that sword with extraordinary prayer rather than self-pity and worry (Philippians 4:6), but also with the knowledge that Jesus himself gave us the blessing of his salvation at unimaginable cost—and with literal nails and thorns.

This is a great resource that Christianity provides to parents. It is the example of Christ, who shows us that to nurture life always takes sacrifice. Those who wish to see civilization continue and love increase welcome the sacrifices that come with new life. This book is addressed to them.

If you give your children to God, cultivate their hearts in community, and accept the sacrifices of parenting with prayer and grace, your children may find themselves contemplating the second "new" birth by the Holy Spirit. To that we turn in the next two chapters.

Second Birth

Now there was a man of the Pharisees named Nicodemus, a member of the Jewish ruling council. He came to Jesus at night and said, "Rabbi, we know you are a teacher who has come from God. For no one could perform the miraculous signs you are doing if God were not with him."

In reply Jesus declared, "I tell you the truth, no one can see the kingdom of God unless he is born again."

"How can a man be born when he is old?" Nicodemus asked. "Surely he cannot enter a second time into his mother's womb to be born!"

Jesus answered, "I tell you the truth, no one can enter the kingdom of God unless he is born of water and the Spirit. Flesh gives birth to flesh, but the Spirit gives birth to spirit."

—JOHN 3:1–6

This is the most famous and substantial text in the Bible telling us about the "second" or new birth. Let's ask this passage several questions about being born again. Who is it for? Where is it from? What does it do? How does it come?

Who Is It For?

What does the average American think when they hear the term "born-again" Christian? They usually think of a particular type of person. People know that some folks are more emotional, they seek a cathartic experience and want to raise their hands and sway as they sing their hymns. Fine, they think, that's the type of person who likes born-again religion.

Others may think of people who need a lot of moral structure. They may have had broken lives, having fallen into addiction or other kinds of life-dominating problems. This sort, it is often said, may benefit from a regimented, structured kind of religion with lots of absolutes and rules. That's another kind of person who needs born-again religion.

Finally, in our society, "born-again" Christians have a reputation for voting for politically conservative candidates. The reality is certainly more complex, but the public image leads to the same kind of conclusion. To be born again, it is thought, is something only for a person of a certain temperament, life experience, or brand of politics.

The trouble with this whole view is seen in Nicodemus himself. This chapter in the gospel of John gives us an account of a man who comes to speak to Jesus at night. We are told a lot about him in two brief phrases. He was "a man of the Pharisees" and "a member of the Jewish ruling council," known as the Sanhedrin. From these two facts we can deduce a number of things about him. As a member of the council he would have been an older male of the ruling class. As a Pharisee he would have been not only moral and religious, but highly self-disciplined.

He was not, then, an "emotional type." Nor was he someone whose life had collapsed and who needed more moral structure in his life. He was a Pharisee—the very epitome of moral structure.

Was he, however, a superconservative type? You might think so, but consider his startling portrayal here. He is at the heart of the establishment, a gatekeeper of the leading cultural institutions of his day. Yet here we see him coming to Jesus—a man who had never gone to the rabbinical schools, who had no academic or political credentials, and who came from the lower rungs of the working class. Yet Nicodemus respectfully calls him "Rabbi," and seeks to learn from him. This shows not only enormous generosity of spirit but also an unusual open-mindedness.

So who is Nicodemus? He's a moral, successful person, but also as open-minded, tolerant, and generous a man as you could hope to find. He is neither a broken person who needs structure, nor an emotional person who needs a cathartic experience, nor someone of a prejudiced, conservative temperament. And yet it is to *him* that Jesus says, "You must be born again."

He does not say, "You know, Nicodemus, you are a pretty good man in many ways. You have a lot to your credit, but if you just add these practices and these duties you can be right with God." No, the message is that nothing he has done so far has actually moved him any closer to God at all. Jesus says, "If you want a relationship with the King of the world you have to be completely remade from the ground up. You must be born again."

Jesus's call cannot, therefore, be a call to dysfunctional people to adopt structured morality and religion. It's actually a *challenge* to morality and religion, because that's what Nicodemus represents. Jesus is subverting the patronizing idea that the new birth is only for a certain type of person. And if salvation is based on the new birth and not on attainments, then anyone can be born again.

Jesus's point is radical but simple. Everyone needs to be born again because no one can even see the kingdom of God without it. That's who the new birth is for. It's for everyone.

Where Is It From?

In John 3:3 Jesus says you have to be born again to see the kingdom of God, and in verse 5 he says you must be born again to enter the kingdom of God.[1]

Remember that Jesus is speaking to a Jewish Pharisee. What would the "kingdom of God" have meant to Nicodemus? It would have meant the resurrection at the end of time, the new heavens and new earth that Isaiah promised (Isaiah 65:17, 66:22). As a team or organization riven with conflict and dysfunction becomes a cohesive unit under a good leader, so when God returns to the earth at the end of time the presence of his full kingly power and glory will put everything right.

Many Greek philosophers believed history was

endless and cyclical, with periodic great purges in which the world burned and was cleansed, after which history started afresh. They had a technical term for that. They called it the *palingenesia*, which means the regeneration or the rebirth of the world. But these "rebirths" were never final. They started things over, but history always inevitably moved into decline.[2]

Yet in Matthew 19:28, Jesus takes this technical Greek philosophical term and uses it in the most startling way. He speaks of "*the* renewal of all things [*palingenesia*], when the Son of Man sits on his glorious throne." He is saying that the philosophers had it wrong. When he returns to rule there will indeed be a regeneration of the world, but it will be once and for all. It will not merely wind things up in order for them to run down again, but it will destroy all evil and death and wipe away all suffering and tears.

That, of course, is an amazing claim in itself. But in Titus 3:5–6, when Paul is talking about the new birth, he says, "He saved us through the washing of regeneration and renewal by the Holy Spirit, whom he poured out on us generously through Jesus Christ our Savior." In English that is not so striking, but the Greek word for "regeneration" is *palingenesia*. So Paul is saying directly what Jesus is hinting at by tying the new birth to the kingdom of God.

Even though the kingdom of God and all its infinite power to cleanse and renew will only come fully at the end of history, the new birth is an implantation of God's future power into your life *now*. The future glory that God will show forth at the end of time to heal everything in the whole world can come into your life now, partially but actually, and begin to change you from the inside out.

So where is the new birth from? It's from the future! I'm sure you are surprised that the Bible includes a message that is more often associated with time-travel stories, but here's a piece of time-travel *non*fiction. The new birth is not a matter of us going into the future; it's the future coming into us. It's the time that's traveling, not you. It is the power of God to regenerate the world coming into your life now to begin to slowly but surely change you into the image of his Son (Romans 8:29).

That all might sound very abstract, so let me show you one very practical implication. Never underestimate the power of the new birth for change. Look at Peter—he was cowardly and spineless. Look at Paul—he was rigid, harsh, and cruel. Yet the new birth made one as courageous as a lion and the other like a tender shepherd, and turned them both into world-changing figures. And were they made of more promising raw material than you or me? They were not. There is no hurt or fear, no guilt or shame, no weakness or flaw—there is nothing in your life that the new birth cannot remove and begin to heal.

What Does It Do?

The most essential feature about the new birth is what it does to the person who experiences it. From Jesus's words we learn that the new birth is, as we might expect from the metaphor, the implantation of new life.

In John 3:5 Jesus says we must be "born of water and the spirit." Many people read that as meaning we need to have two things in order to be saved: we need to have faith and to be baptized.

But it is much more likely that Jesus is talking about only one thing. Bible scholars point out that Jesus is referring here to Ezekiel 36, in which the Spirit of God is likened to water because in arid, desert climates, water was so necessary for survival it virtually *was* life. In short, the new birth is the implantation of God's very life—the Holy Spirit himself—into you. What does that mean? There are certainly many things we could say if we would roam all over the New Testament. But we will confine ourselves to the metaphor Jesus uses here—of being born like a child out of the womb into the world. To be born again means at least two things that are implied in this image—new sensibility and new identity.

The first is that in the new birth we receive new sensibility.[3] Jesus says you need to be born again to "see" the kingdom (verse 3).

All living things, even plants, have some way

to sense their environment. Human beings, of course, have their five senses, and when a child is born she is bombarded with new sensory experiences of light, sound, feeling, smelling, and tasting. It must be overwhelming.

In a similar way, the new birth brings a new spiritual sense. It is the ability not only to intellectually grasp truths about God, yourself, and the world that never made sense before, but also to feel those truths in your heart in a completely new way. To be spiritually alive means you can sense spiritual realities because now you have spiritual sight and taste. One of the very first places this change becomes obvious is in how you read the Bible. You may have been raised going to church and Sunday school and have known various Bible stories and even memorized many verses. But after the new birth, you start to see connections and truths in the Bible that you never noticed or that you may have assented to mentally, that now move, comfort, and illuminate you in ways you had never experienced before.

You had heard "God loves you" or "God is holy and just" or "God watches over you," and you may have agreed with some of them as propositions, but now they become life-transforming realities that shape your daily life and actions. You begin to see implications you never dreamed of. "Wait!" you may say. "If this is true about God—then why do I feel like this? Why do I behave like that? I don't have to be like this anymore." Archibald Alexander, the first teacher of theology at Princeton Theological Seminary in the early 1800s, speaks about it this way:

> Every man, on whom this divine operation has passed, experiences *new views*

of divine truth. The soul sees, in these
things, *that* which it never saw before. It
discerns, in the truth of God, a beauty
and excellence, of which it had no conception until now.

Alexander very quickly insists that, even though
this new spiritual "sense and sensibility" is true
of all who experience the new birth, we must not
expect that it dawns and develops identically in
each person. He writes: "Whatever may be the
diversity in the clearness of the views of different
persons, or in the particular truths brought before the mind, they all agree in this—that there
is a new perception of truth."[4] No one can insist
that these new perceptions come in the same
way. Sometimes the change may be dramatic,
sometimes very gradual. Also, it is not this or
that particular truth that always comes home to

the newborn person. This new spiritual sense can operate in an enormous variety of ways.

Still, there are some commonalities. One of them is to hear believers say, "I'd heard this all my life, but it never made sense before." In particular, people declare that Jesus's love in dying on the Cross for them has finally become palpable, melting, and beautiful. "Like newborn babies long for the pure milk of the Word,"[5] writes the apostle Peter in 1 Peter 2:2. Biblical truths go from being words on a page to being food and drink that you relish and that become part of you.

Here's a striking example. Years ago I was in a committee of ministers that was examining young men who were going into ministry. We asked each of them to tell us something of how they had come to faith in Christ. One after the other said something like this: "I was raised in the church, but I never heard there the gospel preached that you are saved by sheer grace." They then went on to explain how they had finally heard the gospel through some other ministry. At one point, after one more candidate had said the same thing, one of the senior ministers in the room told a story.

He said that he too had been raised in the church and at one point had even tried to study Christianity by taking some educational courses, including one in which he had to learn about Martin Luther and read excerpts from his famous commentary on Galatians. A couple of years later, when he was in the military, a chaplain explained the gospel to him. He realized that he had always thought being a Christian was trying to live like Jesus, and if we did that with sufficient sincerity and diligence, we would go to heaven. But now the chaplain explained that salvation was by sheer grace through Christ's work on our behalf—his life, death, and resurrection—and our salvation could be received once and for all in an act of faith. Gratefully and joyfully he took that step of faith with the chaplain.

Then he asked the chaplain why no one had ever told him the gospel before. "And," he added, "I don't know why Martin Luther didn't know the gospel."

The chaplain looked puzzled and asked him why he would say that. He replied, "Well, I read his book on Galatians and I didn't see it in there." The chaplain quietly suggested that he go back and reread the book.

"I did," he said, "and there on nearly every page—underlined and highlighted by me—there was the gospel." He hadn't been able to see it—his spiritual eyes had not been open. He concluded his story: "Right now there are people in my congregation, under my preaching, who are not hearing the gospel—because at this point they still do not have 'ears to hear' that come with the new birth."

New Identity

Besides a new spiritual sight and sense, the new birth brings a new identity. That fits with the metaphor of a new birth. To be born as a child is to be born into a family and to receive a name. So John 1:12–13 says:

> Yet to all who did receive him, to those who believed in his name, he gave the right to become children of God—children born not of natural descent,

nor of human decision or a husband's
will, but born of God. (John 1:12–13)

To be "born of God" is no longer to have a name
or identity based on either "natural descent"—the
social status or family pedigree of the traditional
culture—or "human decision"—the achievement
and performance of the modern meritocracy. Instead it is to have the "rights" and privileges of
being God's child. It's a new sense of self and
worth based on God's fatherly love and his identi-
fication with us, all secured by Christ's work, not
ours. That is what we are born into when we are
born again.

What does that mean practically?

To be "born again" means not to become just
an improved person but a new one. Paul writes
that if anyone is "in Christ" he or she is a "new

creation" (2 Corinthians 5:17). He does not mean that literally everything about us changes when we are born again. Rather something radically new comes in, and everything that has been within us changes places, as it were, and is reconfigured.

In a famous passage Paul says that "in Christ" there is no Jew or Greek, male or female, slave or free, for all are "one in Christ" (Galatians 3:28), and yet that does not mean these distinctions are obliterated. New Testament scholar Larry Hurtado writes:

> [Christians'] . . . ethnic, social, and gender distinctions are to be regarded as relativized radically, [for] all believers of whatever ethnic, sexual, or social class are now "one in Christ Jesus." But . . .

Paul did not treat these distinctions as actually effaced. So for example . . . he persisted in referring to himself proudly as a member of his ancestral people, a "Hebrew" and an "Israelite" . . . but he also insisted that "in Christ" . . . these distinctions were no longer to be regarded as *defining* believers in the ways that they had functioned before.[6]

The "newness," then, of the new birth is not that all the various features of your life—your gender, nationality, social class, and so on—pass away. Rather, none of them function any longer as your chief identity factor. They no longer serve as your main significance and security, or as the main makers of your self-regard and self-definition. With one person her nationality ("I'm Irish") might be less of an identity factor than her vocation ("I'm a successful lawyer"). But for another Irish lawyer, it is the nationality that is a greater source of pride and meaning, and so he feels more solidarity with others of his nationality than of his profession. For a third person it is her social activism that is her main meaning in life, and so she feels more unity and pride not in others of her nationality or vocation but with those of her politics and justice work.

In every case, however, there is something that we are most proud of, something that enables us to feel confident that we are good people, that our lives are justified. In Christ, this is what changes. All other Identity factors are matters of performance or pedigree, and they not only make us insecure, lest we not live up to the standards of our pursuit, but they also tend to make us tribal and cold toward those who do not share our identity.

The gospel, however, is radically different. First, it gives us a unique, transformative new self-understanding. It tells us we are so lost and incapable of pleasing God that Jesus had to die for us, but we are so loved that he was glad to die for us. On the Cross our sins were put on him—he was treated as our life record deserves—so that if we put our faith in him, we receive his righteousness; that is, we are treated as Jesus's life record deserves (2 Corinthians 5:21). God now loves us "in Christ," as if we had done all he has done. He loves us "even as" he loves his Son (John 17:23). That becomes the deepest foundation of our identity, meaning, and self-view, demoting but not removing all the other things that are true of us.

At first one might think that this would just make Christians one more tribe who looked down on those without their truth, but that is to forget what that gospel truth is. The gospel says we are deserving of death but saved by sheer grace. The only people who are saved are those who finally admit they are not spiritually or morally better than anyone else. However, salvation by grace does not only humble—it lifts us up at the same time. James 1:9–10 says that Christians who are economically poor "should take pride in their high position," but believers who are rich or well off "should take pride in their humiliation." Let's unpack that a little.

Ordinary identity is either up or down, depending on performance. If your deepest pride is found in your ethnicity or family, then the performance of others in your tribe—or of you yourself—will bring either honor or shame to the whole. There will be times you are bursting with pride and other times you will be humiliated. If your identity is the traditional Western one based on your individual achievements, you will again be either up or down.

But the Christian who has embraced the gospel has received a message that we are sinful and in ourselves worthy of condemnation, yet loved perfectly and unconditionally in Christ and free from condemnation (Romans 8:1). That means we always have a low position *and* an even greater high position in our minds at the same time. James points out that, at various times and in various situations, it is good for Christians to dwell more on one of those truths than the other. If you are poor and have been told all your life you are worthless, then the high position that comes with the gospel should be meditated on constantly in order to heal your soul. But if you are successful and have been getting accolades all your live, then you should think long and often about the low position that comes with the gospel.

This new identity, then, really is a "new creation" that changes everything. It changes our attitude toward people of other races and classes—no longer does our own race or status so dominate our identity that we look down on anyone. Our new "low" position enables us to listen to and learn from people we previously would have despised. But our new "high" position enables us to take on challenges or to speak out and go up against wrongdoing or to testify to our Christian faith—all in ways that previously we would never have had the inner strength to attempt or even the desire to do.

How does the new birth actually bring about this shift? The first feature—new sight and

sensibility—is crucial to this second one of identity. If a lonely and unhappy child in an or-
phanage is simply told he has been adopted by a
wonderful family, that won't change him. He
has to meet them, be hugged by them, be loved
and cared for by them day in and day out. Only
then will the legal change in his name be trans-
lated into a new inner happiness and security.

In the same way, the moment we put our
faith in Christ, we become legally children of
God (John 1:12–13). But that will not reconfig-
ure our hearts and our actual functional identity unless, through the new presence of God's
Spirit, we actually sense his love, holiness, glory,
and reality. Paul says that when we give our lives
to Christ, the Spirit of God comes into our
heart, "and by him we cry . . . 'Father.' The Spirit
himself testifies with our spirit that we are God's
children" (Romans 8:15–16). As we participate

in ordinary Christian practices—of reading the Bible and hearing it preached, of individual and corporate prayer, of building each other up in Christian community, of participating in baptism and the Lord's Supper—the Spirit makes our new identity real to our hearts and we change, slowly but surely. Put in the language of Saint Augustine, the new birth begins to "reorder your loves." You don't love your family or career or people less, but by the power of the Holy Spirit you learn to value God's love more and more.

When I was a young pastor I remember counseling a woman whose life had been changed by the gospel. As she told me her story, she could remember at least four different stages in her life. When she was a young girl growing up in a very strict church, she said to herself, "I know I'm somebody special because I'm more moral than all my friends." The trouble was, of course, that when she slipped up in her behavior, she hated herself because the very basis of her self-worth was disintegrating. Then she moved into a stage of life in which she said to herself, "I know I'm somebody special because this great guy loves me." If anything, her instability increased. She said, "Not only was I emotionally high or devastated depending on whether I was noticed by men, but I stayed in relationships I should have broken off but I was afraid to."

After several years she found some friends who rightly chastised her for taking her identity and happiness from male attention and romance. But then they added that her self-worth should be based instead on her having her own career. She embraced their counsel, working hard on her education and career. Now she said to herself, "I'm somebody because I am a successful

person, making good money, and accomplish-
ing things in the world." But she added, "Now I
found whenever I had a bump in my career
path that it just destroyed me the way the romantic bumps used to destroy me."

Then somebody came along to her and said,
"Oh, you don't need all that to know you're somebody. You just need to know you are a good,
kind person who helps others." And she said, "I
threw myself into helping. I threw myself into
volunteer work. I threw myself into listening to
anybody who had a problem. I threw myself
into trying to help emotionally needy people get
better, until I was so tired. And I hated myself
because I was supposed to love these people,
and I didn't even like them "

In her identity shifts, she went from "I'm somebody because I'm moral—because I'm beautiful—
because I'm successful—because I'm helpful,"

until she finally realized that in every case she was trying to save herself, and she was exhausted. She said, "I realized what I really needed was to know God loved me because he loved me and because of what Jesus had done. That changed everything."

The new birth is not, "I've got weak self-esteem and I need a boost from God." The new birth isn't a sort of vitamin supplement that adds the vague idea of "God's love" to the mix of all the things through which you are achieving your self-worth. Being born again not only changes *what* you look to as your highest good but *how* you look to it. Your heart rests in Christ's freely offered love for you—it does not work for it. It's an identity based on an entirely new foundation.

There is a story (probably a legend) about Saint Augustine. He was converted after having had many relationships with women. One day he was walking and one of his old mistresses came up to greet him. He was perfectly courteous but somewhat distant. She was puzzled. As he politely said good-bye and began to walk on, she said, "Augustine! You know it's me, don't you?" He turned with a smile and said, "I know, but it is not me." Things that had mattered the most to him no longer drove and mastered him. He had a new inner fullness instead of needy emptiness. He had been born again.

How Does It Come?

I've been talking about conversion—turning to God in faith—and the new birth as if they were the same thing. Theologians over the years have made a helpful distinction here. In one sense these two things might be said to be two sides

of the same coin, because they always come together. Jesus says in Matthew 18:3 that "unless
you are converted . . . you will not enter the
kingdom of God,"[7] and in John 3 that unless
you are "born of the Spirit" you cannot enter
the kingdom of God. If both are absolutely necessary, then it follows that no one is truly a
Christian, a citizen of God's kingdom and a
child in his family, unless both happen.

But while the Bible constantly tells us to put
our faith in God, it nowhere tells us to give ourselves the new birth. How could we? That violates
the metaphor. The regeneration of the heart, the
implantation of the Holy Spirit, is not something
you can do any more than a baby can decide to
be conceived and born. And yet turning to God
in faith *is* something we are called to do. Conversion is what you and I do to come to God, but
the new birth is what God does within us.

So the real question is—how do we turn to God so we can be born again? There are two parts, and they are implied here. The first one has to do with grace. The second one has to do with Christ himself.

First, we must turn away from our sins and efforts to save ourselves. Jesus says to Nicodemus in John 3, "You must be born again." Then in John 4, we're given a great example of Jesus calling a woman to conversion, a woman who is the exact opposite of Nicodemus. It's not just that he's a male and she's a female. The point is, her life has been a complete ruin and his life has been a complete success in the world's terms, and yet Jesus calls them both to be saved by grace, as a gift.

When we moved to New York in the late 1980s, Manhattan was a much different place than it is now. Once a month I used to speak at a breakfast at the Harvard Club, and when I'd come up from the F train on Sixth Avenue there were prostitutes and drug dealers around. Then I would walk into the Harvard Club, filled with wood-paneled rooms, overstuffed leather chairs, roaring fires, and everyone looking prosperous and pulled together (and quite a few of them actually were). But the gospel told me then and now that the Nicodemuses in the Harvard Club and the Samaritan women out on the sidewalk were equally disqualified from any salvation based on performance yet equally qualified for salvation based on grace.

The message is this: no matter how good and well-ordered your life is, you *must* be born again, yet no matter how chaotic your life has been or how often and profoundly you have failed, you *can* be born again. Jesus is saying, "You're all on the same level. The most accomplished person and the person whose life seems to be the biggest failure come to God as equals. You are in the same spot. You need to be, and can be, born again." Nicodemus had been trying to save himself with his morality and accomplishments and therefore had been playing God, trying to be his own savior. The woman at the well in John 4 is revealed to have been seeking joy and satisfaction in a series of broken romantic relationships and marriage. She was trying to do the same thing. Yes, it was in a way that brought her social opprobrium, while Nicodemus's way brought him social honor. But in God's eyes, whether you try to save yourself by being moral, or helpful, or beautiful, it doesn't matter. You're trying to save yourself. You're putting yourself in the place of God.

Therefore, everybody—the apparently "best" and "worst"—stands at the same place and on the same level in their need of the grace of God. Babies do not contribute anything to their conception and birth. They don't bring themselves about. They don't get born because they've planned on it. It all has to do with what the parents have done. It has nothing to do with what they do.

Paradoxically, you must understand you can contribute nothing to your salvation in order to receive it. As long as you think "I can save myself. I'm really a good enough person," you are still spiritually blind. You can't see the kingdom of God or experience his grace. This is called repentance—and it's not simply being sorry for this or that sin. This is what the Bible calls "repentance unto life" (Acts 18:11). The first thing you have to do to be converted is to repent before God's grace and say, "I see I've been trying to save myself, and I need your free grace."

The most famous example of this is Martin Luther himself. Here's what he said happened as he was getting converted: "I labored diligently and anxiously as to how to understand Paul's word in Romans 1:17." He was struggling over a verse, "where he says that the righteousness of God is revealed in the gospel." Finally, he says, "I grasped that the righteousness of God is that righteousness which through grace and sheer mercy God gives us by faith. Thereupon I felt myself to be reborn and to have gone through open doors into paradise . . . When I saw the difference, that law is one thing and the gospel is another, I broke through."[8]

There it is. Luther felt like he had been struck with a lightning bolt. For years he knew that he should repent of his sins and get God's forgiveness, but then he thought that he was on his own to pull himself together and give God a righteous life in order to get his blessing and favor. Suddenly he realized not only that he had done sins and bad deeds but that even his good deeds had been done for the wrong reasons—in order to control what God and others thought of him, in order to create an identity for himself of being a good person, in order to save himself and play God. It was when he not only repented for his bad deeds but also for the reason he had been doing all his good deeds that he felt himself "to be reborn." When he realized the difference between the gospel and saving himself through moral effort—he "broke through."

The Beauty of Jesus

So the first thing we must do to be converted is to turn away from our self-salvation schemes in repentance. But then we must turn toward Jesus in faith, seeing the beauty of what Christ has done. It's not enough just to believe in the grace of God in general; you have to have faith in what Jesus Christ has done in particular.

I saw all three of my sons being born, and with each child it was different. They were squalling or silent, kicking or almost motionless. But they all had one thing in common. They were not being born, getting their new life, or being brought into the world by *their* labor. They were being brought into the world through the pain and labor of their mother. We live today in a society in which giving birth is not as painful or life threatening as it used to be. But when Jesus was talking about being born again he was living in a time in which you did not see the light of life unless someone loved you enough not only to experience pain and suffering for you but also to put her very life on the line. Indeed, in those days, many people were brought to life through their mother's death.

That's the reason Jesus later on in the Gospel of John makes a remarkable comparison. In John 16:16 he says, "In a little while you will see me no more," referring to his death on the Cross. Then immediately he says, "A woman giving birth to a child has pain because her hour has come; but when her baby is born she forgets the anguish because of her joy that a child is born into the world" (John 16:23).

Why, when he is talking about his death, does he suddenly bring up a woman in labor? And why does he speak of the painful moment of giving birth as her "hour"? Students of the Gospel of John know that whenever Jesus talks about his death on the Cross he calls it his "hour."[9]

See what Jesus is saying? "Your first birth brings you physical life because someone risked her life, but your second birth brings you spiritual and eternal life because someone gave his life. That someone was me." And if we stay with Jesus's metaphor in John 16 it gets even more wonderful. He says that, in spite of her incredible pain, a new mother is filled with joy at the sight of her child. So Jesus has the audacity to say, "That's just a dim hint of the joy I sense when I look at you. All my suffering, torment, and death I have willingly borne, for the greater joy of saving and loving you." Until you see that and believe and rest in that, you cannot be born again.

Growing in Grace

Simon Peter, a servant and apostle of Jesus Christ: To those who through the righteousness of our God and Savior Jesus Christ have received a faith as precious as ours . . . His divine power has given us everything we need for a godly life . . . He has given us his very great and precious promises so that through them you may participate in the divine nature . . . For this very reason, make every effort to add to your faith goodness; and to goodness, knowledge; and to knowledge, self-control; and to self-control, perseverance; and to perseverance, godliness; and to godliness, mutual affection; and to mutual affection, love. For if you possess these qualities in increasing measure, they will keep you from being ineffective and unproductive in your knowledge of our Lord Jesus Christ. But whoever does not have them is nearsighted and blind, forgetting that they have been cleansed from their past sins.

—2 PETER 1:1, 3–9

*But grow in the grace and knowledge of our Lord
and Savior Jesus Christ. To him be glory both now
and forever!*

—2 PETER 3:18

Jesus's image of salvation as a new birth
was taken up by the other New Testament
writers, by Paul (Titus 3:5), James (James
1:8), John (1 John 5:1), and Peter as well. Twice
in his first letter Peter tells Christians they have
been born again (1 Peter 1:3, 23). One of the
clearest implications of this birth metaphor must
not be overlooked. Human beings do not, like
the goddess Athena in the Greek legend, spring
to life full grown from the forehead of Zeus. We
begin as the tiniest, most helpless babies. The con-
trast of our newborn selves with our full-grown

selves could not be greater. The amount of growth that a newborn must undergo is staggering—he or she must double their size in the first four to six months.

Do newborn Christians, however, evidence anything like that kind of change and transformation? The groundwork for it has been laid, as we have seen. We have the indwelling of God's Spirit. But do we grow?

In Peter's second letter he proceeds to talk about spiritual growth. In both the opening verses and his concluding statement he urges us to "grow in grace."

Growth in Grace Is Possible

Remember who is writing this book—"Simon Peter, a servant and apostle of Jesus Christ" (2

Peter 1:1). Peter was an apostle who lived with Jesus. He saw Christ transfigured on the mountain. He heard the voice of the Father coming out of heaven. He failed Jesus, but then Jesus forgave, healed, and commissioned him to be a leader in his movement. Then, after his resurrection, with the nail prints still visible, Jesus trained Peter personally.

Imagine all that happening to you. We throw the word "life-changing" around too lightly in our culture, but certainly if you had personally seen the transfiguration and the resurrection *that* would have transformed your entire life. But then look what Peter says: "Simon Peter, a servant and apostle of Jesus Christ, to those who through the righteousness of our God and Savior Jesus Christ have received a faith as precious as ours." The Greek word used there, *isotimon*, means "of equal merit and value." How remarkable it is that he writes to Christians hundreds of miles away and many decades after these events that he saw with his own eyes, yet he says that their faith is of equal life-changing value as his. He is saying, "Your life can be as revolutionized by the gospel of Jesus Christ as mine was."

How could that be? Almost immediately Peter explains. Verse 4 tells us that through the "precious" promises (the same word)—the promises of the gospel—we "participate in the divine nature." When we receive the Holy Spirit through the new birth, we get God's DNA, as it were. That does not mean that somehow we mystically merge with our deity, but it means that the love, wisdom, truthfulness, justice, mercy, and goodness of God is instilled in us. The

Holy Spirit connects you to the spiritual character of God the way your DNA connects you to
the physical character of your ancestors.

In the end, it was not the eyewitness experiences that changed the apostles. Remember that
Judas lived with Jesus, saw the beauty of his
person and his great miracles, but still turned
away. Even when the resurrected Jesus appeared
to his disciples on a mountain in Galilee, some
worshipped but "some doubted" (Matthew 28:17).
What truly changed them was the same thing
that all Christians have, the indwelling of the
Holy Spirit (Acts 1:8).

When the Bible calls you to grow in grace, it
is very different than saying, "Be virtuous." Many
have thought that the New Testament is simply
calling everybody in general to base their lives
on the ethical model of Jesus. Jesus was a man
who did love and mercy and justice, they say. If

we all lived like him, the world would be a better place.

With all due respect to the sentiment, the biblical authors are not that naïve and foolish. To call people to live like Christ, to adopt a way of life that goes utterly against our nature through an act of the will, is to ask for the impossible. The Bible's calls to Christians to become like Christ assume they've been born again and they are a partaker of the divine nature. When New Testament writers say, "Love your neighbor as yourself," they're saying, "Nurture that new nature inside you so you can love your neighbor as yourself." You have to be born in order to grow. If you're going to grow physically, you have to be born physically. If you're going to grow spiritually, you have to be born spiritually.

There is no excuse for not having a radically

changed life if you're a Christian. Have you given up on change in certain areas? Learned to live with bad habits and patterns in your life? Have you silently made peace with wrong attitudes, fears, and resentments in your heart? You have "everything you need" for a godly life (verse 3). Growth in grace is now a powerful possibility.

Growth in Grace Is Gradual

Peter speaks about "adding" to your faith one quality after another—goodness, knowledge, self-control, mutual affection—and then says that these must be present in "increasing measure." In other words, growth in grace is gradual.

Our culture trains us to be impatient. A company that can only deliver the product two days from now will be put out of business by one that provides next-day delivery. A computer that takes ten seconds to download something will be put out of business by one that gives us the same features but downloads in two seconds. Bankruptcy over an eight-second difference! That's the kind of culture we live in.

And the church often has been overly shaped by the culture at this very point. Many churches and ministries say directly, or at least hint implicitly, that if you really give your life to Christ and come into our congregation and use our methods of spiritual growth, you will be soon delivered from anything that enslaves or ails you. They promise spiritual victory over your problems as a kind of magic bullet.

But the Bible never talks like that. We are born again—we start out as spiritual babes, as Peter says elsewhere in his letters (1 Peter 2:2). No one goes from being an infant to a functioning adult in a few weeks, or months. It takes years and years of nurture and effort and trial and error—usually very big errors—and learning from everything. The Bible never says (to paraphrase 1 Peter 2:2): "Like newborn babies, drink in the spiritual milk of the Word of God so you may grow up in your salvation. And if you drink really, really, really hard, you'll grow up faster." No, babies grow as they grow. It takes a long time.

And yet. If you take an acorn and you try to smash a giant slab of concrete with it, the acorn will be dashed to bits. But let's imagine that slab of concrete is part of a sidewalk. Plant that acorn in the ground underneath the sidewalk. If it germinates it may find a way to sprout up and slowly, over the years, push that concrete slab aside. It may even crack it in half. That's the power of slow but steady growth.

So growth in grace is less like a bullet and more like an acorn. It comes into your life and if you water it and nurture it, it eventually will utterly change you. If the power of God is in you, it eventually will deal with your greatest weaknesses. If the love of God is in you, eventually it will confront your selfishness. But it is gradual.

It should be kept in mind that, just as growing children do, spiritually growing Christians will show many individual differences. Parents who have more than one child know that they do not all learn their first words, take their first steps, or do anything else at the same age, at the same time, and at the same rate. Even twins differ! And so it is with spiritual growth. Some of us come into God's family having had far more difficulties, mistreatment, and character challenges than others. Some of us also come with little or no knowledge of the Bible or Christian teaching while others come with a great deal, and therefore progress in the Christian life, while always gradual, progresses at different paces for different people.

There is one more way that spiritual growth follows the pattern of a child's growth into adulthood. The great eighteenth-century hymn writer John Newton (the author of "Amazing Grace") was also a wise pastor. In letters to a friend, he spoke of three basic stages of spiritual growth, which roughly corresponded to childhood, adolescence, and adulthood.[1]

Like children, new believers are often enthusiastic and filled with wonderful new feelings of both freedom from guilt and closeness to God. But, Newton says, while they have believed the gospel—that God's forgiveness is a free gift, not earned or deserved—they have not yet learned to apply the gospel to their whole lives. They still are, at root, legalists. They know God has forgiven them, but now they ground their confidence that he continues to love them in their avoidance of major sins, in their faithfulness in prayer and growth in Christian knowledge, and especially in their feelings of nearness to God. All these things serve as the *basis* for their certainty that God loves them instead of the *result* of their certainty that God loves them. Because of this there are currents of anxiety ("Does God really love me?") and pride ("I've given my life to Christ—unlike these stubborn people"). Young Christians become overly downcast over negative feelings and spiritual failures because their feelings and spiritual successes have functioned as their "merit-causes," the basis for their favor with God.

Therefore, Newton notices, God often allows

a period in which many things go wrong in the Christian's life. This corresponds roughly to adolescence, because adolescents can struggle with parental authority. When the spiritual feelings recede and life is going poorly, the "adolescent" Christian veers back and forth between anger at God and anger at himself or herself. But, Newton writes: "By these changing dispensations, the Lord is training him up and bringing him forward."

God leads struggling believers into a deeper understanding of the gospel. Immature Christians believe that the good feelings and circumstances of their lives have been earned through the strength of their devotion to Christ. The subtle (or not so subtle) smugness and naivete is jolted out of them by difficulties and trials. They can move forward when they go deeper into the two truths of the gospel—that they are more sinful and flawed than they had believed, but that their acceptance by God is more unconditionally secure in Christ than they ever had dared hope. As Newton writes of the growing Christian: "The hour of liberty, which he longs for, is approaching, when, by a farther discovery of the glorious Gospel, it shall be given him to know his acceptance, and to rest upon the Lord's finished salvation."[2]

Finally, Newton speaks of mature "spiritually adult" Christians. Because they have grasped the gospel more deeply, they are able to handle suffering well, realizing that evil circumstances do not mean that they are being punished for their sins, or that God does not care. Also, because they now have a more radical view of God's unconditional love for them, they have the emotional strength to be far more honest about their own besetting sins rather than justifying or denying them. In this way they can understand themselves and overcome their character flaws as never before. Newton writes that "[the adult's] happiness and superiority to [the adolescent] lies chiefly in this, that . . . by means—such as prayer, reading and hearing the Word—he has attained clearer, deeper, and more comprehensive views of the mystery of redeeming love."[3]

Growth in Grace Is Vital

When the New Testament speaks of grace it means God's unmerited favor, his willingness to accept you not because of your works and record but because of Jesus's. In one sense, therefore, you can't grow in grace. You can't be more justified and righteous in his sight. You can't be more adopted into his family. But in another sense, you can grow greatly in the influence of these truths on your heart. Your power and experience of these great privileges can increase. When that happens, and only when that happens, you have a dynamic power in your life that changes you from the inside out.

Some years ago we were on vacation and were in a fast-food restaurant, but the service was anything but fast. Our line was moving very slowly because, as we could see, the woman behind the counter was having trouble with every order. As we got closer I could tell that the reason for all the delays was that her English was very poor. She appeared to be a recent immigrant and could not understand what was being said to her. I became impatient and said to myself: "Why did the management put someone in this position without proper language skills?" But then I remembered a Bible verse I had seen that very morning in my daily reading. It was from Deuteronomy, where God was telling the Israelites to be kind to the immigrant and foreign nationals in their midst.

> And you are to love those who are aliens,
> for you yourselves were aliens in Egypt.
> (Deuteronomy 10:19)

I was caught up short. God did not say—though he could have said—"You must love and be kind to immigrants, because I say so!" That would have put pressure directly on the will. While there is nothing wrong with that, it does not create long-lasting change. But God did not frame this command in that way. He is saying to the Israelites, "Remember, I liberated you when you were aliens and slaves. Now treat immigrants and aliens as I treated you." That doesn't merely pressure the will; it changes the heart, humbling and yet building up with a remembrance of his love. That is not calling for mere ethical compliance. It requires growth in grace—having the logic of God's grace permeate your thinking and change the motives of your heart.

And of course I instantly knew that this applied to me as well. I was never a literal slave in Egypt, but as Saint Paul wrote, I too had been "excluded from citizenship" in God's kingdom and one of the "foreigners . . . without hope and without God in the world. But now in Christ Jesus you who were once far away have been brought near by the blood of Christ" (Ephesians 2:12–13). Jesus did this by losing his power and place in heaven so that I, a spiritual foreigner and outsider, could be brought in. He was excluded so I could be included. Long before any modern talk about "checking your privilege," God provided every believer with a powerful antidote to our natural tendency toward racial and class superiority.

And so as I stepped up to the counter to speak with her the thought came to me: "Lord Jesus, I too was an alien, but you brought me in at infinite cost to yourself."

When you understand grace, it begins to change your heart and it begins to nurture the new person God is growing within you. The result is real patience, real kindness, and real behavior change.

See what we mean when we say that growth in grace is vital, from the inside out, organic rather than mechanical? You can grow a pile of stones by throwing more and more stones on the pile. In the same way you can heap up Chris-

tian activities and perfect attendance at church.
You can even grow in head knowledge of Christian doctrine and biblical facts. But that is not
the same as growing wiser, deeper, happier, and
more loving.

Are you growing like a pile of stones, or are
you growing like a child becoming a mature
adult? Growth is possible. Growth is gradual.
Growth is gracious and vital.

When Growth in Grace Is Actual

What does growth in grace actually look like
when it is in progress? Archibald Alexander gives
us this list.

There will be overall progress despite occasional lapses. Our growth will be sometimes
faster and sometimes slower. It will be stronger

in one area than another. But there will be—
over time—advance.

There will be a growing unselfishness, an ability to check one's indulgences that cost other
people, especially family members, much grief.
This means the advance in your ability to control
your spending, eating, and your tongue in public. Alexander adds, interestingly, that "the coun-
terfeit of this is an over-scrupulous conscience,
which sometimes haggles at the most innocent
gratifications."[4]

There will be sometimes a feeling of God's reality in both corporate worship and prayer, and
an increasing desire to meet with him in such
times of devotion. This certainly waxes and wanes
depending on many factors. Illness, weariness,
trials, and difficulties, or other times of heavy
busyness and activity, can lead to a decline in
what the older writers called "God's sensible

[sensed] presence." But overall there must be continual though intermittent seasons in which we commune with God in love through prayer and reading his Word. The famous hymn by William Cowper describes this:

> Sometimes a light surprises
> The Christian while he sings;
> It is the Lord who rises
> With healing in His wings;
> When comforts are declining,
> He grants the soul again
> A season of clear shining,
> To cheer it after rain.[5]

There will be an increasing love for people who are hard to love, a willingness to involve yourself in the common good of the community through loving your neighbor, and a willingness in particular to identify publicly as a believer, sharing your faith in the hopes that others can eat the same food on which you are living.

An especially strong evidence of growth in grace is when you can bear mistreatment from others by forgiving them from the heart and by desiring their welfare even as you fearlessly but humbly seek justice and the righting of any wrongs.

There will be growing reliance on the wisdom of God in the twists, turns, and circumstances of life. Romans 8:28—that God causes "all things to work together for good to those who love God"—does not claim that every individual evil thing produces some good, but it does promise that *together* all things in your life are being fitted into a pattern, mostly unseen by you, that works for your benefit and his glory. Christians who depend on this promise find that "however dark may be your horizon, or however many difficulties environ you . . . you have learned to live by faith. And humble contentment with your condition, though it be one of poverty and obscurity, shows that you have profited by sitting at the feet of Jesus."[6]

Finally, a sign of growth in grace will be increasing love for other Christians, and not just those of your particular human tribe. Sadly, the Christian church is still divided in large part by race and class, so it is likely that you go to church with people of your race, educational level, and social class. But a great sign of growth in grace is that you discover a closer bond with a believer of a different social status than you do with nonbelievers of your own. This love for other Christians, when genuine, breaks through the barriers of politics and ideology, race and class, that divide all other human beings.

Have you seen these kinds of changes in your

own life—this new sensibility, new identity, new habits, new loves? Slowly but surely they should be growing in and changing you.

For one of the most intriguing examples of this new creation we can return to the figure of Nicodemus, this time looking not at John, chapter 3, but what the gospel tells us about him at the very end of the book, when Jesus dies.

In John 19, when Christ's dead body was still on the Cross, Nicodemus and Joseph of Arimathea, two wealthy, successful men of the Jewish council, come and ask for the body of Jesus. Then they go to the Cross and take the body down. After that, we're told they dressed the body themselves—they prepared it for burial. They cleaned it, wiping off all the blood and filth. Then they lovingly wrapped it and put sweet-smelling spices within the burial garments. Their actions were shocking. Why?

First of all, it was a bold move, unbelievably courageous, because when the leader of a movement is being executed, you don't want to be seen as one of his followers. Indeed, all the other followers had gone into hiding, yet these two men were willing to get up and identify clearly as his disciples.

Also, it's important to know that the only people in that culture who washed and prepared a dead body for burial were women or slaves because it was considered (and it was) a foul task. Men of high rank would never do such a thing, but Joseph and Nicodemus did.

What this means is that something had changed drastically in Nicodemus. On the one hand, he was more courageous and brave than he had ever been before. And yet, on the other hand, his masculine pride was gone. He was both bolder and humbler, more courageous and more culturally flexible than he'd ever been before. Where did this redeemed masculinity come from? It came because his whole identity had been pulled up and replanted in new soil, the soil of the gospel. As we have said, the gospel takes you both lower and higher than any other belief or experience can take you. If you are saving yourself, you are bold if successful but a bit arrogant, or if you are failing, you are humble but lacking confidence. The gospel tells you that you are a hopeless sinner in yourself but in Christ saved and loved through grace. That makes you what you see here in Nicodemus and Joseph—bold and humble, strong and tender—all at once.

The paradox of the gospel is that only those who admit their complete weakness get this strong, and only those who, as it were, "lose themselves" actually "find themselves" (Matthew 10:39). C. S. Lewis ends his book *Mere Christianity* describing it.

> The principle runs through all life from top to bottom. Give up yourself, and you will find your real self. Lose your life and you will save it. Submit to death, death of your ambitions and favourite wishes every day and death of your whole body in the end: submit with every fibre of your being, and you will find eternal life. Keep back nothing. Nothing that you have not given away will ever be really yours. Nothing in you that has not died will ever be raised from the dead. Look for yourself, and you will find in the long run only hatred, loneliness, despair, rage,

ruin, and decay. But look for Christ and you will find Him, and with Him everything else thrown in.[7]

The Blessing of God

Hebrews 6:7–8 tells us that life and growth come from "the blessing of God."[8] So, readers, my prayer is that you will live under that divine blessing.

The birth of a new baby is a wonderful event. Congratulations!

The birth of a new life in Christ is an eternal event. Hallelujah! *Born once, die twice. Born twice, die once.*

Now "grow in the grace and knowledge of our Lord and Savior Jesus Christ" (2 Peter 3:18).

Acknowledgments

For this book and the series of which it is a part, we owe even more thanks than usual to our editor at Viking, Brian Tart. It was Brian who saw the short meditation on death that Tim preached at the funeral of Terry Hall, Kathy's sister. He proposed that we turn it not only into one but three short books on birth, marriage, and death. We also thank our many friends in South Carolina who made it possible to write this and the companion books while at Folly Beach last summer.

Notes

First Birth

1. Derek Kidner, *Psalms 73–150: An Introduction and Commentary*, vol. 16, Tyndale Old Testament Commentaries (Downers Grove, IL: InterVarsity Press, 1975), 502–3.
2. Christy Raj has done some interesting work on gender in C. S. Lewis's Space trilogy, which you can access here: *withhandsopen.com*. I recommend all her posts, as well as a careful reading of *Out of the Silent Planet*, *Perelandra*, and *That Hideous Strength* for some of the most challenging and helpful reflections on masculinity/male and femininity/female ever written.
3. Jennifer Senior, *All Joy and No Fun: The Paradox of Modern Parenthood* (New York: Harper-Collins, 2014), 43.
4. Senior, *All Joy and No Fun*, 44.
5. Senior, *All Joy and No Fun*, 8.
6. C. S. Lewis, *Prince Caspian* (New York: Macmillan, 1951), 182.

7. The majority of Christian churches in the world—Eastern Orthodox, Roman Catholic, Anglican, Lutheran, Presbyterian, and Reformed Methodist—practice infant baptism, but of course there are hundreds of millions of Christians who do not, who only baptize persons who are old enough to make a conscious profession of faith. We will not here try to make a case for infant baptism. Rather, we believe nearly all Christians will understand and practice, in one form or another, the basic spiritual move of both Israelite circumcision and Christian infant baptism—the move of offering your child to God, bringing them into the community of faith, and praying for and expecting his grace to come into your family for the task of parenting.

8. There are several versions of these questions online. They have obviously been altered for use in different churches, and it is not possible to tell which ones are the most original. I've given a representation of the slightly different forms.

9. Kim Tingley, "What Can Brain Scans Tell Us About Sex?," *New York Times Magazine*, September 18, 2019.

10. See James D. Hunter, *The Death of Character* (New York: Basic Books, 2001).

11. See Hunter, *The Death of Character*, Part Three: Unintended Consequences, 153–227. "There is a body of evidence that shows that moral education has its most enduring effects on young people when they inhabit a social world that coherently incarnates a moral [cosmology] defined by a clear and intelligible understanding of public and private good . . . where the school, youth organizations, and the larger community share a moral culture that is integrated and mutually reinforcing. . . . Needless to say, communities with this level of social and cultural integration and stability are scarce in America today" (155).

12. Alasdair MacIntyre, *After Virtue: A Study in Moral Theory* (South Bend, IN: University of Notre Dame Press, 2007).

13. These two views are well laid out in Kenneth Keniston and the Carnegie Council on Children, *All Our Children: The American Family Under Pressure* (New York: Houghton-Mifflin Harcourt Press, 1978).

14. Timothy Keller and Kathy Keller, *God's Wisdom for Navigating Life* (New York: Viking, 2016), 285.

Second Birth

1. It's important to consider that while the term "kingdom of God" is used constantly in the Synoptic Gospels of Matthew, Mark, and Luke, the Gospel writer John almost never uses the term. This is the only place, outside of a fleeting reference near the end of the book, where he mentions the term at all. This means the new birth in the New Testament is closely tied to the concept of God's kingdom.

2. "The term *hē palingenesia*, 'the rebirth' . . . [is] a term which is more typical of Stoic philosophy than of Jewish writers, but which aptly sums up the [Old Testament] eschatological hope of 'new heavens and a new earth' (Isaiah 65:17; 66:22, etc.). . . . In Stoic thought παλιγγενεσία was the term for the cyclical rebirth of the world as it rose from the ashes of its periodic conflagration." R. T. France, *The Gospel of Matthew*, New International Commentary on the New Testament (Grand Rapids, MI: William B. Eerdmans Publishing Co., 2007), 742–43.

3. This section is heavily dependent on Archibald Alexander, *Thoughts on Religious Experience*

(Edinburgh, Scotland: Banner of Truth Trust, 1967), 21–31.

4. Alexander, *Thoughts on Religious Experience*, 64.

5. New American Standard Bible.

6. Larry Hurtado, *Destroyer of the Gods* (Waco, TX: Baylor University Press, 2016), 93–94.

7. New American Standard Bible. The word "converted" is used here in the KJV and NASB translations. Other translations say merely we must "turn," but the Greek word *straphete* means a complete revolution from going one direction and turning to go in another direction. Jesus says that this turning means that spiritually we "become like children"—humbly trusting. This is why Bible scholar Leon Morris writes: "In this context it [the word *straphete*] will signify a change of direction of the whole life, a conversion." Leon Morris, *The Gospel According to Matthew*, Pillar New Testament Commentary (Grand Rapids, MI: William B. Eerdmans Publishing Co., 1992), 459.

8. Martin Luther, "Preface to Latin Writings," in *Luther's Works*, vol. 34 (St. Louis: Concordia, 1972), 336–37.

9. "'Hour' (*hōra*) constantly refers to his death on the cross and the exaltation bound up with it

(7:30; 8:20; 12:23, 27; 13:1; 17:1), or the consequences deriving from it (5:28–29), so it would be unnatural to take it in any other way here." D. A. Carson, *The Gospel According to John* (Leicester, England; Grand Rapids, MI: Inter-Varsity Press; W. B. Eerdmans, 1991), 171.

Growing in Grace

1. John Newton, *The Works of John Newton*, vol. 1 (Edinburgh, Scotland: Banner of Truth Trust, 1985), 197–217. The letters we are examining are the first three—"Grace in the Blade," "Grace in the Ear," and "The Full Corn in the Ear." As can be seen even by the titles of the three letters, Newton uses a number of images to describe what he calls A, B, and C Christians. I am here using only the metaphor of child, adolescent, and adult.
2. Newton, *The Works of John Newton*, vol. 1, 203.
3. Newton, *The Works of John Newton*, vol. 1, "On Grace in the Full Corn," 211.
4. Archibald Alexander, *Thoughts on Religious Experience* (Edinburgh, Scotland: Banner of Truth Trust, 1967), 159. Alexander adds that some

people go to such legalistic lengths to exercise self-control that "some do hesitate about taking their daily food" (159).

5. *William Cowper's Olney Hymns* (Minneapolis, MN: Curiosmith, 2017).

6. Alexander, *Thoughts on Religious Experience*, 160.

7. C. S. Lewis, *Mere Christianity* (New York: Macmillan, 1960).

8. "The soil enjoys the benefit of *rain* frequently showered upon it for its enrichment and fertility, so that it in turn may by its fruitfulness be of benefit to others. In fulfilling this function it is blessed of God. Spiritual productiveness is a manifestation of the operation of divine grace; for it is God who sends the rain of his mercy upon the soil of human lives, and who also as the husbandman tends his vineyard (Jn. 15:1) and gives the increase (1 Cor. 3:6f.)." Philip Edgcumbe Hughes, *A Commentary on the Epistle to the Hebrews* (Grand Rapids, MI: William B. Eerdmans Publishing Co., 1977), 222.

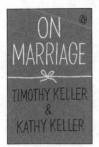

Ready to find your next great read? Visit prh.com/nextread